The lyric here is both cry and love song. ... cry for the beloved, knowing the beloved ... .stand transformation better than death, though / I practice for it every night, with you." Transformation in language is metaphor, the magical force that moves substance to spirit. Again and again Gravendyk enacts this magic, a gift for those who will grieve, which is all of us: "I fluttered in your chest, and was remembered."

JULIE CARR, author of *Rag*

What happens to the lyric voice when the air pushed from lungs through throat and mouth becomes more precious as it becomes more faint? These poems are not restrained by the illness of a poet taken from us too soon, but rather are energized by an abiding interest in the special kind of presence, of the embodied phenomenology that illness makes possible. To state this as Gravendyk's philosophical orientation is to state a particular kind of courage, one that discovers curiosity in tragedy and renders etherial the kind of heat and density produced under the most crushing of pressures. In delicate lyrics then, these poems synthesize defiance and resignation, building toward intensities that obtain clarity at the most precarious of moments.

JOSEPH JEON, author of *Racial Things, Racial Forms: Objecthood in Avant-Garde Asian American Poetry*

In Hillary Gravendyk's astonishing, posthumously published book of metamorphoses, both body and language enter into the cycles of transformation. The reader follows her keen vision into the strange and unsettling territories these poems traverse, and like some latter-day Keats she teaches us both "the downfall" and "the jubilation" inherent in the fact that we are "forever bound to our bodies," "which flower and fail." These are poems of relation, the I tenderly addressing a you, and they were in their composition already aware of the unfathomable distance they would ultimately have to cross. "I was a long time away," Gravendyk writes. These final poems return her to us anew, and will bear her indelible vision far into the future.

JESSICA FISHER, author of *Inmost*

the soluble hour

THE SOLUBLE HOUR HILLARY GRAVENDYK

OMNIDAWN PUBLISHING
OAKLAND, CALIFORNIA
2017

Cover art by Jean Nagai
"Hear and Now II" acrylic on canvas 2017
Instagram: @jean_nagai

Text set in Century Gothic and Adobe Jenson Pro

Cover and Interior Design by Sharon Zetter

Offset printed in the United States
by Edwards Brothers Malloy, Ann Arbor, Michigan
On 55# Glatfelter B18 Antique
Acid Free Archival Quality Recycled Paper

Library of Congress Cataloging-in-Publication Data

Names: Gravendyk, Hillary, 1979-2014, author.
Title: The soluble hour / Hillary Gravendyk.
Description: Oakland, California : Omnidawn Publishing, 2017.
Identifiers: LCCN 2017020876 | ISBN 9781632430458 (paperback : alk. paper)
Classification: LCC PS3607.R383 A6 2017 | DDC 811/.6--dc23
LC record available at https://lccn.loc.gov/2017020876

Published by Omnidawn Publishing, Oakland, California
www.omnidawn.com   (510) 237-5472   (800) 792-4957
10 9 8 7 6 5 4 3 2 1
ISBN: 978-1-63243-045-8

CONTENTS

INTRODUCTION

Hillary Gravendyk was an exceptionally insightful and loving poet. Her love of nature emphasized the botanical flux of minutiae at hand and she held the landscapes of California and the Pacific Northwest close in her imagination. She had at her disposal the energies from a childhood full of time outdoors and steady encouragements. She had an intelligent heart gained from the life she'd lived and fiction she'd read, sharpened by a savvy ear. Her work explored ideas of navigation and orientation: no reason to question love or bodily limitations exactly but every reason to observe pain's transformations and alchemy of love and the body. The poems she made from a life of medical procedures, embodiment, and love stands as some of—if not the finest—poetry about illness written in American letters. Her imagination generously pushed outward to the world, making salient metaphors out of desert, sea, and an unperturbed voice delivering even the greatest fears: That there will be no long years in which her new poems arrive is for us the loss of a major American poet.

At nineteen, Hillary was given a medical prognosis of six months to a year to live; her case was a statistical outlier as very few people were ever diagnosed that young. She lived to be thirty-five. I asked her widower Benjamin Burrill if Hillary was born with her willingness to suck the marrow out of life or if it came from her illness. He said "Yes." While she would find eleven p.m. the perfect time to dig apricots out of the fridge to make jam, or relish a delicate lotion she'd encountered, her conviction on how things should be beautiful gave her patience with poems. She allowed time for words to come to maturity. Her access to emotional clout coupled with this willingness to wait ensured her published work was stunning. Among her poems, you'll find what happens when a tremendous lyric voice has to sit with its own mortality too closely from late adolescence until adulthood. The poems found unpublished in any volumes after Gravendyk's passing are presented here without line edits, rather only judicious ordering and inclusions and only the most obvious of typographical corrections. I am grateful to Rusty Morrison at Omnidawn not only for making this book possible and for being the kind of editor Hillary appreciated, but for feeling strongly we shouldn't tamper with these poems: On this point she and I wholeheartedly agreed.

The majority were from a dropbox file titled "second book." Hillary hadn't yet chosen a title and so I vetted *The Soluble Hour* with Benjamin and with her mother Katherine and both agreed this was suitable. It is the title of one of the poems included in this work. To me, this title suggests some of the qualities and complexities of time, which Hillary could so masterfully interrogate. Hillary had found the pitch in her lyric voice that could wield all of her poetic gifts to evoke a sense of time as being both too short and eternal. Further poems were found in files on her desktop, poems with personal dedications and known to be recent; after consultation with Rusty, Benjamin and Katherine a few older poems were included and a slight few of the newer ones were omitted.

In 2008, I met Hillary at the Vermont Studio Center. On that first day of our friendship, Hillary told me about her illness and what her prognosis most likely was—that she might live longer but not into old age and that she would require a lung transplant. I think I deeply and instantaneously accepted this fact. We immediately began to collaborate, making up challenges for each other and writing poems back and forth. When I was home, I sent her many playful and ridiculous limitations to see if she wanted to collaborate by e-mail. This was always fun. It is not surprising at all that Hillary has had many writer collaborators: her sister Megan Gravendyk Estrella, Maureen Alsop, Colleen Rosenfeld, Brenda Hillman, myself, and others. She made friends easily and recognized each person's best qualities.

While at Vermont Studio Center, we spoke about Agnes Martin and art. We were there with Rebecca Carter, a fine arts/ fiber artist who was relocating to Dallas at the time. Rebecca talked about the importance of being seen, of understanding each other, and Hillary expanded on this by saying that when she saw Agnes' paintings, they moved her because of the tiny swerves or signs of human life within the structures she so carefully built. It seemed Hillary was not attracted to art that matched the furniture, for sure: she wanted to be challenged by a vision. I looked that week at her manuscript, at her request, and I was fascinated by the authority she had over fragments and the tiniest details that were a phenomenon that might have gone unnoticed even by an acute writer. She had no qualms about saying something was letting her down aesthetically. How many of us who knew her recall her cooking something and saying, "It needs something." And I think this discernment allowed her to create poems that exerted wisdom through astonishingly seen details: her fragments made themselves into landfalls of understanding. These insights transmitted and created spaces fertile for seeing things as they are yet somehow were luminous with her love of the world.

Hillary and I both applied to the Vermont Studio Center that spring in order to study with the poet Alice Notley. Hillary texted me that she knew Alice had arrived from Paris because she spotted Alice in the cafeteria eating toast. This text made me run from my studio to Hillary's to fangirl with her in person. It was so important for us, Notley's certainty of her own vision, her free intimacy with her mind and the voices in it. Notley's artistic impulse goes beyond confidence and intention to something very matter-of-fact and elemental. Hillary's inspirations and intellect were so engaged with the sensual and social world (the sweater, the tangerine, the friend) that perhaps for her, Alice Notley's presence amounted to a confirmation that--whether in the external or internal world—more is more even if living in a human body is a quandary.

We had a laugh after our conferences with Alice; she'd held up one of Hillary's drafts and said, "it goes". Hillary and I found a dozen ways that week that an outfit or a sentence satisfied us—"It goes," she would say with a spark in her eye. And so here, we—Benjamin, Katherine and John Gravendyk, Rusty Morrison from Omnidawn, and I—have tried with all our hearts to give you the poems Hillary left, and to give them to you in the way we found them: poems easily transmitting this spark of elemental intimacy—poems that afford the reader acceptance and love, "it goes"—that was Hillary's essence as a person and a poet.

Cynthia Arrieu-King
Philadelphia 2016

For Benjamin

AMAZONITE

you cast

a handful of shadow

against a bare tree

strike a warrior stance—

your jade eye opalescent

your skin filmed with white—

thick with small noises the forest

crouches around you

animal loosed in the dead

leaves you pick up the scent

I laid down for you.

My cabochon tongue clicks and

your hand twitches open an abandoned

nest threaded with glass

you're just out of reach

behind a fir, in the dark mouth

of the vale, buried in a shallow river bed—

the light sequins the floor

the wood closes around you.

COMING BACK

I was a long time away.
The summer sky rinsed with clouds.
Confetti rain. No one saying goodbye, no
one waving from the deck of an ocean
liner. Walking away like going down
the aisle. A perfumed avenue
of blown flowers. Anticipation streaming
like a banner across every face. Your hand
a prediction; my hand
a delectation. Raspberry-lipped summer,
I gave you up like a loose promise. Never chose
to come back. Something like a hand
darkening my chest. And visitations, rosy
with care. Bound by a heavy love, I came to stay.
The knuckle of hard belief worried to a smooth
finish. House with its keyhole architecture
of small spaces held apart. I tampered
with a chambered heart, I stuffed my mouth
with opal. I glistened at the rim of any hour,
I turned my fingers on a burning lathe, pressed
my skin into the sinuous heat. I
was a long time away.

ATTACHMENT

In that half-light, your face. Who told you to climb into that bright
unsteadiness, cleaving to dream as a mussel clings to searock?
An eye-line darkened with ash. Attachments clutter the room:
buttonhole dangling with charms, box that sighs and growls. Your
hand surfaces from the black water, slick and open like a bird's wet
wing. Call me back from someone else's precipice. Creosote summer
burning with assurances. Your mouth a protected field, your hand a
soft barrier. A solar system of sparkling bruises. We've collected failed
remedies: tree bark, belief, saltwater, bay leaf, lemon, refusal. Pain
lit up like a traveling circus. You look at me in the bathroom mirror,
press your face into my hair.

THE SOLUBLE HOUR

Pocket garden of eden, peach-mad, plum-ridden, tampered:
a dress peeled away like a tulip blade, cliché of its single blossom —
mouthed into some lush berry, rose-burdened, round.
Once in water, once in woods, once before we shut the door.

Rescue each rustle from the cling and slip, unbottled shade
a spill of nape and rushes. The soluble hour, the granulated hour
the hour resized for sleep. Our mouths were bird-thirsty, crackling,
the sheet unrolled like an echo: my skin, skin, kin —

tree sculpted from pink drifts of shadow. Forty visions
in a single night, and for the eyes there were cherry pits
licked clean. How it feels to be the bloom in your hands how
to be taken clear down to the stone — to be sweetened into bareness.

FAIRY TALE

I taught the downfall and I taught the jubilation
I taught the carriage horse, sleepwalking its route

I taught the promise and I taught the incantation
Taught a three-part harmony, whistled or sung

I taught the screech owl its chilling abiding
I taught the target, the arrow, the bow

I taught the looking glass its double rotation
I taught the preen, the powder, the slice

I taught the truth and I taught the mistaken
I taught the gathering and the suspension

I taught you a message to carry in winter
Taught you the waters that rustle and creak

I taught you the break in the night's celebration
Taught you the gorge and the justified sinner

I taught you the secret, the mystification
Taught you the candle the bell and the book

I taught you, at last, a story for tellers:
Loss always has time for you, if you wait.

QUARREL

I was an observer of longing. Caught the glint from the green
harbor light and argued for love. I was the delicate dictator, sipping
Gin Fizz and spilling champagne. Sleek shoes spattered by night-
wet grass, cars that looked like carriages. Wondering when you
had gone up the staircase to the uncut library. Someone bustled
inside the butler's pantry, someone laughed like a bell on the lawn.
I was a hopeless suitor, clutching the hem of your long blue skirt,
offering you cigarettes. There was the tale of perfection and the
tale of disaffection. They mingled like guests until they could not
be divided. I was the storyteller, stumbling on separation. Along
the lakeshore silted with lights, a hand running along a spine. You
were absent at your own celebration, called away to the juniper
grove. Fingers ringed with glass. You said your own voice was full of
pennies; I scoured the grounds until I learned what you meant.

HILLARY HILLARY

You creep through the air, a voice calling my name
in this dimmer winter where keels freeze to swells
I was lost in the delicacy of your warning, at sea.

Held myself against the roll of your tongue,
the door open like a mouth and the air falling
through more air, a hole in the light—

You carry each pinprick of rain and lay
me in fragments on the counterpane,
you circle the room, a quieting crow.

The window slices absence into segments
the door slaps the side of the house
and I'm ankle deep in clouds.

[MACHINE OF GRASSES]

Machine of grasses, unrolling every spear into the rockface. A pell-mell, clockwork-meadow, furled against the backs of my eyes. A thousand minute hands, sweeping into the wind.

My eye slips like a jewel from the scene, into another, lidded field, one bracketed by weather, or the threat of weather. I fall back into a pillow of earth, hands throbbing with purpose.

Don't be afraid for me—*when the wind takes me it takes you, too*—a flag of leaves bannered in the dull air, a small bird skirting the tips of ticking pine needles. Stop drifting out of range.

Your body like a streak of sun, smeared across my face and my chest. The hairs rise up on my arms, like tall grass.

Meadow of every occasion, an alarm about to ring, an eye closing, an eye opening, a fringe of fingers, combing your hair, a stalk hollowed into a green straw, my hand, marked by yours.

[I CARRY YOUR TASTE AS IF IT WERE A STONE]

I carry your taste as if it were a stone. Not your skin, but what it touches, what it fails to touch. We take in a scene from the front steps, rinse it of color. Then birds rush from your throat singing and falling, singing and falling. It's the inside of a dream, the air gray as a dead TV, the screen transected by wings. Follow the arrows out of my heart. Nothing guides you like the thing that leaves you, nothing stills your hand. The room a size smaller than the room before. It's a sign of misfortune, I think, shifting a handful of gravel into the pocket of my dress. The return message. You laugh and your body crumples like a page. You feed me need and I open my mouth to receive it.

SOMETIMES, WHEN ALONE, I HEAR MY NAME

Ghost ring tone and someone saying my letters or claw-hammer
or gentle. Caller I thought I knew you. Slipped through a heavy
snow into a heavy sleep. Mossed belly, strewn hillside, earlobe. The
bedroom crowded with stillness, the air full of names. The river
was fastest near the banks, the boat drifted into a net of weeds, we
laughed but were shaking with cold. Window-sash eyelids, stopped
against storms. Now on the soft carpet I'm bound by rumors I tell
myself, algae twined around each wrist. From a Rock-thrust throat,
the bellow of water. I might as well admit I've lost you a thousand
times. Shelled spine along a sandbar. Nest of brown hair and nettles.
But you find me in every landscape. Back curved against a bitter
wind, grit in my hair, hand tracing the only name I hear.

SUMMER STORM

Silent streak of light
and the water quickly rifled
like the pages of a book
your body a quiet island
in a quieter sea.

radio tuned to static
that scribbles in the air
that blooms into black
and scatters

you try to catch hold of it all
the camera's eye flickers
voices scratch against the pink
night, papered-out moon

banked against a cushion
of neon clouds, the wind
a charcoal scarf wound around
the shore's neck

wings out like a wet
cormorant you'd stand against
a darker backdrop, the still heart
of fullness, the steady drop

of a beating tree—branches failing

against their disappointed wood—
your rush and whistle, your
promise your require—I'm

waiting, ringed with rocks
and purpose, Daphne at the water's
edge, the stag on the hoof, your hand
raised against rain, ready to strike.

THE SLEEPER

The loosely shrouded hour darkens the room. Limbs like an
archipelago on a sea of white foam. A cry released like a balloon,
then quiet.

Fledgling wanderer makes a thin passage through dreams, my own
breath haunts the air, then black trees fold around us.

No path to the front door, the mail slot open like a mouth, no
turning away from this small sustenance, this momentary expiration.

A blue shadow slips across the afternoon: another day emptied of
promise, of the idea for promises. Sleep is softest in the cradle of a
litany of things undone.

Sound nestled in the chest's white wound. Unblinking, dynamite eye
held open against the ice-white day, against the cold lid of meaning.

THE LONG GOODBYE

There's a pocket in my dress
filled with seeds,
I'm flush with heat, with you
waiting for them to flower

Bent against eventualities
you've slumped into my bed again
hands stressing the distance between
my body and yours.

Make no promises, though I do it
all the time. You return but pretend to be
gone. Kiss me as though you were
teaching me a lesson
in restraint.

It's an unpretty nightscape, starless
and shadowed with creatures that move
away from us. A tree in the path breaks
the path in two.

THE WOMAN IN WHITE

Hung a piece of white flag from the shoulder. Clump of grass sprung under a pointed boot, creamy and spattered with wet road. The white white ankle, the bandaged knee. You kissed the letters of a tomb. Error in a cloudy language, a red warning someone wrote across the sky, folded into a pocket square, left fluttering in a splintered post. There was a light rain in a churchyard. The moon a blue smudge on a soft black cloth. Locked away they grow wild and anxious. At the crossroads, a long story, half-told. She was a tall woman dressed like a little girl. Some say patient, some ghost. Landscape that refuses to forget.

WHERE ABSENCE GOES

The winter you lived in India
I sought you where you'd left—
among those you kept close
there was a patch of green eye
nearly yours, spread like a meadow
half hidden by night trees there
I pressed two fingers behind
another's ear, forging a secret nape
where the mark left would be
yours or its mirror, mine

& was kissed—
there in the creeping wood
he with your name, saying it, me
holding the sound like the crook
of an arm until we turned away
from each other, skin cool
to the touch, a packet of
soundlessness passed from
one palm to the other palm.

THIS IS CALLED DIVINATION

In the last dream, the horses were shod with bone. You prodded my
chest with a divining rod. The riverbed thwarted the bright water.

At the end of the beggar's highway, we hung a celluloid sun.
Knew the way four clad feet left the ground: quatrains
        of little moons. They rose and fell, but quickly.

Rain gemmed the fading sky; the air caught its breath.
Imagine a padlock made of flesh, imagine it was yours.
Imagine what is locked behind it, behind the star of cobalt blood,
clotted at the catch.

The nights fanned out like a deck of cards. You stood behind
a pillar of wind and were quiet. I was as small as a small brown bird.

There was the distant thrumming of hooves, there was your pulse.
There was you who found the lost spring, cool and secret. I fluttered
in your chest, and was   remembered.

AT THE RETROSPECTIVE

Our eyes fold the light into a box so white so full
of every trapped sound in the squared darkness
around us. I feel your hand in my hair like a spark
settling among firs, a droplet of heat that could
light up or lay waste to us. We turn the corner
into a room clouded with a pink softness we nestle
into, another couple is so busy wondering if they've
missed it that they miss it. The pink bundles itself
into a cumulous inner sky and then a cherry tree about
to break into blossom — as Wright's body once was, as
my body would do if I could make it. It's not that I'm
too happy for our beloved bones, it's that
I understand transformation better than death, though
I practice for it every night, with you. I wonder what
you would break into, for love.

TRANSIT OF VENUS

Toward what blackness tracing
the inner contours
of what sun? The flares
curl and drift, the hair
around your face I
am rummaging through clouds
to find you.

Heliotropic heart always
straining, the water-glass
prism freckled with shadow, the
smoke from the brown
hills. A fir tree closes
its one eye, my eye.

Along a burning path, a hole,
a place to stumble or disappear—
or a pupil, dilated, staring back
at the upturned faces
in a pebble of dark
washed with so much light.

OCCASION POEM

for Megan and Stacey

I dreamt an unlabeled map of this strange country
we share. Your hand in mine like a letter
in an envelope; something you sent me to guard
against suffering, a rush of breath exhaled into
my chest, a book of hours we wrote together—

You said *see the state that looks like a door?* And
I did. Not California, not Washington, this door
was familiar as my skin. On the other side
were stars, one for every word you spoke to me,
every word a brightness in a darkened sky—

And it was you who dreamt the map of this day forward:
your soles weary, your compass true, your heart
always offered to your loved ones
with both hands

FOREST FLOORS
for Claudia

Folded inside the word is the wood. Tree totems, patch of earth, bird sound. Nothing is quieter than a wild place in our chests. The word for "air" in an animal language. The fir needle's fresher wick pulling blood to the surface of the hour. Our betrayers grown into the scenery, taut against the skin. Some tithe with grasses, the pinecones piling up like drifts of dry snow. Some swim in the cold ocean, falling on rocks, picking kelp apart, dreaming of redwoods and gnats swarming over deep lakes. We'll all come to concluding phrases, full of river-washed stones, full of soft moss. Forever bound to our bodies, which falter, which spring up fern-laden groves, which flower and fail.

SARDONYX

Black of the bruise that spirals from the eye--lilac, goldenrod,
mint—a scented bouquet smeared across your skin: war palette.

I wove grasses into the dead wings of uninvented birds, crushed
berries into blood so that the eye would reanimate the woodland of
your face—

cast-off smile, a coal cabochon in the hand, or smooth ash on the
tongue. You tasted your wound, wore it like a diadem,
        the crown of every hour.

YOUR GHOST

Parted from the scene of old disasters
a magnet pulling one memory in two directions

the hand stilling the circles in a puddle
mind placed against the side of a stone

I guess we haven't offered up any new truths
turned your heart inside out for pennies

braided your hair into a soft basket
held nature's charms at arms length

wondering who sleeps where at night
where the imprint of your body goes when you rise

your ghost spilling like a lake into the hall
flash-flood of absence and promise

the sight of every angled enmity a kiss on the brow
the slope, the axis, three points in a bucket of lines

I know these roads by heart and all the ways back in
an arrow strung up like a party favor points the way

I want to hear your voice at the bottom of the stairs
I want to get drunk, hit rock bottom, kill something small

I want to break every heart in the room: your apparition
curled around my neck like an animal
made from clouds.

QUIETING

We've combed these fragments
for images

arranged a gallery of glyphs & signs
to show where we read
& where

to make corridors of mirror
and ink, to make
the hashmark of reading

into a quiet muzzle
for an eye's darkened hallway—

reflectionless / sure.

We might find our wrists
among these leafy bracelets

close / flowering

or arrive at a dark portrait

of another's face
flustered with ice or
blooming.

Outside the growing
is less selective

we forest
thickly / vacantly
like snow

outcroppings spreading against
themselves or else against
treacherous softness

What arranges such a season?

a pocket of orange glare
opened in the spine?

a ribcage loom starred
with melted snow?

What nudges a blue gleam
from a white hollow?

Some steadier hand might
reveal a truth
gin-clear / quaking—

but that bracket of arms is
the buried rope in a quieting blizzard

the long line we wait in
& then turn to face, tenderly

We may become those
pictures of ourselves in time

wintry skin rimmed with lamplight
clothing folded into black lines

our faces
wondering / scudded with shadow.

THE NATURALIST

The blow fly enters houses, but is senseless there,
lays eggs in the bodies of fruit, then feeds.
nerves blare bright as sirens, harden in winter light:
dished red eyes, metallic blue-bead abdomen, clear wings.

On the tongue, rotted taste warms
spit and sugar shard the rim
of what is tightly gathered
into bone—

Blue-bottles enter the house, and each collection teems
with a disarray to swipe at; now a wave is frustration, now hello.
tiny clocks divide the hour into tiny hours. alight:
bottle of seashells, discarded familiar, metallic bead.

The air stiffens like a predator
rooms snap and tick underfoot:
salver of frozen lake crossed
with fractures.

There is no natural habitat, but outside of it you lose bearing
have trouble measuring distances, circle in the mirrored hall.
abandoned, the stone room is glossy with purpose:
ring of chairs, slack mouthed window, clear wing that is

folded into a glass box;
nothing as stark with detail
pinned at the expanse
of motion—

& WHAT COVER

No division this time—

fringes rest frayed   rustling
gridded fields plangent   with rain
& scummed with grey-light
This is the kind of promise   you don't keep—
markers are thick with mud   & horsetail
straggling   & yellowclover
They will still remove.

Nearish the riverbed   bracken woven tight
like an overturned basket   underside of each leaf
furred   soft peachskin
woven nettle   bundles of blood colored fruit
limbs   quilled   & hairy with rain
They cleave   to their cooling –

pushing inside vines   staple
themselves   to the tracery skin
of the wrist   a clutching then
there is wet grass   blackness wet
This is a childish moment

buried in leaves   somewhere an
overturned bucket   here a
hole   & points   & berries

& what tiny   what thronging—

so much water   highway far away here
as a sky   which whistles   which thickens
there along the edges   all the favorite lines—
shush of cars   still audible   in this hinged landing
between things   & what berries   sound
what black   what puncture   & what   cover—

BURIED SHORELINE

woods threaded with smoke   shredded

sky mist furling through   needles

of trees these   woods are wooded   too.

snuffling dog rooting   water   gooey rocks loon   sits long along

one long   leg   a shore   edgeless   tumbling into ocean then

trickling green patches   as river   bed and there are

rivers   buried under rotten   logs

Peaks shorn   in swathes, twinned   against something grey that

might be weather   or   a kind of cloth.

a sound like a low   cry   a cry

we are moving between these lookouts   the shore the

forest   a   sense of watching   through   car windows

they are   each finger   each   other nail   crudded   damp

red splinter of bark   milled with   moss wet soil

and on the same bed   tiny shells

dead mollusk husk when the rock is lifted   white   as gull

shit   or mooncrater   fossilized droplet canyon   made fast these rocks   dried sea   charcoal blue   if we lifted a red

log   shedding   softly along the grain of itself

would there be teems   of beetles   crushed snailshell

mushrooms   dry sand pink   and blue ?

driftwood flares up   like candy   pulled across   an outpost of

coastlines   crusted   on moving water and we find

more coast slid   under the deck

clam trails erase   wetly   the sandspout candlewax at the palest

touch you   think you are   the master of looking keep   looking

AS IF AN ECHO

I'll be
    suspense of weather between milky mirrors
                                cloudmud caught blearing

              Some fine-ness of   pine
                limb   bristles in limb

ANSWERS TO SENSUAL QUESTIONS

Some of the time   what glows in late light
           or moves against the blades of gate-wood
       or grass
         is not
           what happens:
always again   seeds blow and suspend, alight
      in whatever motes become, at rest

      what's seen
          describes you:
       variable for place~

The light rustles,
      disputes the hillside in early Spring
           circles a jelly-jar of still water,
                tumbling. And down
                      the fire-road of suspicion, clues:

~
Elsewhere and here   automatic nature unsoiled by growth
                  ground silver with the mechanisms
                      of freighted things
                        managing flight
such solutions   dispel into a bright stillness
                pick the heart's lock and there is only light,
                    weed furrows,

                    something late,
                    and moving

UNCONTROLLED SMILE

bowing out of it, the tree limbs scatter their
passerbys along the sidewalk, blurred through the
shop windows, seeded with scraps of paper, scotch tape
the erasure of moving faces. out of the open blue doorway
across the street a thick woman with a bottle of tomato juice
isn't controlling her smile, it is working
frantically along the seams of her face, eyes squinting, neck
bumbling forward—the smile so bright and stretched
it is the very cusp of weeping. a bag of nickels
or b-bs the pressure behind
eyes unsealing, the air bright and unconcerned flutters aimlessly
though the spikes of frustrated hair,
threading the unsealed eyelids and their tiny
spider-star lashes. If anyone
could look at her, she could be beautiful, or look back, or
settle into a rhythm of ticks and
winking, a blur, perhaps, a stillness

THE ROWERS

Garland of bruises
adorn the bone and tendon
at the hinge of my rising and falling, at

the keelboat's waking hour
still as held breath. but sharp
with cold air, cold horizon lined with

a slim row of shadows that
snaps forward then reclines
against the smudged sky, against

abstraction. grey air
rises along the shore's arch
and along the tender spine, along

the fragile vein, it pools,
loses its breath and turns black
under the skin, a skimming under

the rower's crooked arm
lifts the silhouette into its own wind
extends a dark arrow, fluently extends

a flap of water
streaming away in the very moment
it unfolds its wing, smoothly unfolds

the morning's first sound
keening across the channel to return,
stroke for stroke, the same small wounds.

NOW SUN, NOW SURFACE

Now in the lidded field a bird   shifts wildly

       across the burdened sense we wait for
   across a brown wing

and under an eye
beneath a hill
a cluster of sweetened dirt
a daisy made of rough sensation
a facing out.

Have we been here   falling into control   comets
lunging for oblivion

    in each slippery husk   another sameness

    taped to the back of our hearts—

a minor boldness
a flat of crowding

out   where a rib moves like a sparrow   inside a light
and grassy heat   ?

There is partition   from the air
and blank lacery.

Wring our torsos out   blacken a knuckle with charred
tree   or sleep

          outside a fogbank   blurred with silica dust.
Do not answer

the sound of the tightened sun
the hatching wire screen
our own creatures   hollering
musky with healing.

DIORAMA

III.

Inside, things are sizeabley arranged, each
to a season. They may appear quietly and more
elaborate than they are, but sheltered against
the elements, how could they appear otherwise?

Against a rosy pane and a rough wall, a hand
might be pressed—rudely or with delicacy—might leave
a mark combed with prophetic lines or else a blurred
star of heat, fading at each finger-point. In such a long hall
"goodbye" gets repeated until it becomes our politest greeting.

IV.

Decoratively we skim forward, studding streets
that fold themselves into cul-de-sacs, elaborating patterns
in the perforated sky. Each display repeats, hosts subtle
alterations. Here we describe desire as a numbered series

Where the light is trimmed into a retractable holiday
and glass bulges with what passes, what is preserved—
But let's say that that clanging is a moving train:
one should always be reminded of being left.

BY EXPOSURE, BUT GENTLY

Each capture buries itself deep
inside a cloud of fading:

a track swings clear and erases

a mouth tunneled with snow.

We've packed and repacked
tiny, glistering burdens

into quieting hours swollen with
fragility, with a peculiar softness.

This vantage is arranged by
jutting absences:

tall rods signal into a stiller blur

soundlessness is a bluer flare.

We become our own conductors
to bow, stiff with cold; shift aside

each curtain of our white and ashy hearts

and empty onto another blinding hillside
another buried depot muted with this

light & gritty blank:

only to appear again, bent cold

over what we've preserved in ice.

Along a waist-deep border, flared
sharp as a bullhorn, anguished
scratches mark the fogbank:

trees bare as matchsticks or

something captive— falling.

WHISTLE STOP

This could be poised between
trains moving   at two speeds
that eventually meet

in what city   at what hour

past the sawmill, fish-plated track
makes a junk terminus of uncoupled cabin
cars and coal-black engines buried in grass

She says *ignore the trains.*
She means   *answer the question.*

above, lyric with its tiny numerous folds
rigs delicate spiral staircases   that imitate
little snowflake moons for flecking "ties" and "spikes"

then   below a white slope:

on the surface of Crater Lake
real wood ducks, jade slices of moon
behind each eye, hang

And once upon a time, a meteor careened
from the sky in pinwheels of light
made an empty space between   two shards of mountain

She says *ignore the moon it makes.*
She says *ignore the lake.*

clean gray perspiration of rock and peak
stippled the inside of the blast   then ran together
streaming veins the way water   blooms into a sudden body

after all only the lake is beneath the lake.

In the foothill town
a darkened whistle hollows out the air
as it moves forward   signaling the train
and *the train.*

THE SECRET OF INSET LIBRARIES

You're pressed along the ledge   and gathering
spores against storms.

A november flood
blooms like a harness

                                    over the shellacking

banks

                                    over the blood stained

water gauge

our aureate girdle slumps

over the memorized pasture—

                and you've plunged a wet hand
                    into a cluster of paper
                    into a rifled bed

                                    our hungry animals
mewling

                into bundled softness, warm as a papercut

You've slid a hand behind the fireplace   humming and

      removing an error
      this isn't a latch
          it's a tunnel of keys
          it's a cruor drawer

               our cellophane skin crimped at the
seams

it's a confusion—
          one breath to another
          each prepped and legible

                something swabbing the
perimeter

plus our unhurried pulse
buried in salt.

FIRST COMPASS

Some called it courage
what felt like blindness:

peering into cupped hands to keep
from seeing how sea and sun

split a sky into bright halves.
It was only something we traded:

the sensible horizon for a bauble,
a pocket earth, constantly measured,

a cipher wound tight as a clock;
it may as well have been a strand of blue beads.

We believed familiar stories: traced rows
of animal stars, drew charts studded with claws—

in the evenings we ate hard-tack
and traded superstitions like worn coins.

Winking, we shifted with the shifting sea
steadied ourselves along the black

line between stillness and motion. And
our compass opened like a locket:

inside was a heart, pierced and pointing
through the wet night— ignorant

of the icy polar moon, the eye's white
axis, the long and shortened lines of the palm.

POSSESSION

Too many milky summers
burdened with blown roses

and finch calls press borders
out of grass and covered-porch

houses sided with children
darkly seeking one another—

a smocked arm leans pale
into the bare wood palette

that has no underneath
beneath its uprootable frame.

Small scrap of pinched light
along that sideyard filled

with interior: who watches shyly
these nostalgic transactions?

The Brother in the afternoon, the
unseen Mother stilling play or

our own eager, museum-boxed
eyes? This record is incomplete

but inside that chamberless square
another copy of another face—

there is a granted door
through the stairwell of passing

breath; at the casing a bracket
of burned pages moves stiffly

and in a mirror the color of Scotch tape,
flushed with camera light, there is

the soft girl leaning away from
the soft girl, leaning away.

ACKNOWLEDGEMENTS

Gratitude to the editors of journals in which some of these poems originally appeared: *comma, poetry, DUSIE, Newfound, Sugar House Review*.

Profound thanks to Hillary's teachers: Lyn Hejinian, Brenda Hillman, and Robert Hass. Sincere thanks to all of Hillary's colleagues at Pomona College including Colleen Rosenfeld, Kevin Dettmar, Claudia Rankine, Kyla Wazana-Thompkins. Thanks to Joseph Jeon, Jessica Fisher, Julie Carr, and Alice Notley for their support of Hillary's work. Special thanks to Rusty Morrison, Ken Keegan, Gillian Hamel, and Liza Flum at Omnidawn for all their hard work and care both for this volume and for Hillary's first book, *Harm*. Warm thanks to Hillary's parents Katherine and John Gravendyk, her sister Megan Estrella, to Benjamin Burrill, and to her many beloved friends. I'm sure this space would include, if she were here, Hillary's gratitude for you, her deep love, and her wish to be with you all.

BIOGRAPHY

photo by Benjamin Burrill

HILLARY ANNE GRAVENDYK was born in Los Angeles, California on March 1, 1979, and grew up in the Snoqualmie Valley of Washington State, near the town of Carnation. She attended Tulane and the University of Washington and went on to get a doctorate in English Literature from the University of California, Berkeley. In 2008, her chapbook *The Naturalist* came out from Achiote Press and in 2011, her book *Harm*, published by Omnidawn, was a finalist for the California Writer's Exchange Award. In 2009, she was hired to teach 20th Century poetry at Pomona College in Claremont, California. After moving to Oakland in 2003 with her husband Benjamin Burrill, Hillary lived out most of her adult life in the San Francisco Bay Area and Claremont.

CYNTHIA ARRIEU-KING is associate professor of creative writing at Stockton University. Her poetry volumes include *People are Tiny in Paintings of China* from Octopus Books, *Manifest* from Switchback Books, and *Unlikely Conditions* from 1913 Press, written with Hillary Gravendyk.

The Soluble Hour
by Hillary Gravendyk

Cover art by Jean Nagai
"Hear and Now II" acrylic on canvas 2017
Instagram: @jean_nagai

Text set in Century Gothic and Adobe Jenson Pro

Cover and interior design by Sharon Zetter

Offset printed in the United States
by Edwards Brothers Malloy, Ann Arbor, Michigan
On 55# Glatfelter B18 Antique
Acid Free Archival Quality Recycled Paper

Publication of this book was made possible in part by gifts from:
The Clorox Company
The New Place Fund
Robin & Curt Caton

Omnidawn Publishing
Oakland, California
2017
Rusty Morrison & Ken Keegan, senior editors & co-publishers
Gillian Olivia Blythe Hamel, managing editor
Cassandra Smith, poetry editor & book designer
Sharon Zetter, poetry editor, book designer & development officer
Avren Keating, poetry editor, fiction editor & marketing assistant
Liza Flum, poetry editor
Juliana Paslay, fiction editor
Gail Aronson, fiction editor
Trisha Peck, marketing assistant
Cameron Stuart, marketing assistant
Natalia Cinco, marketing assistant
Maria Kosiyanenko, marketing assistant
Emma Thomason, administrative assistant
SD Sumner, copyeditor
Kevin Peters, *OmniVerse* Lit Scene editor
Sara Burant, *OmniVerse* reviews editor